BIRDS OF PREY

photographs by
Simon M. Bell

text by
Pauline Beggs

SOMERVILLE HOUSE, USA
NEW YORK

Copyright © 1998 Somerville House Books Limited.
Photographs © 1998 Simon MacDonald Bell.
All rights reserved.

No part of this publication may be reproduced, stored in any retrieval system or transmitted in any form or by any means, electronic, mechanical, photocopying, recording, or otherwise without the prior permission of the publisher.

ISBN: 1-58184-002-0 A B C D E F G H I J

Illustrated by Julian Mulock
Art Director: Neil Stuart
Design: FiWired.com
Printed in Hong Kong

Somerville House, USA is distributed by
Penguin Putnam Books for Young Readers,
345 Hudson Street, NY, 10014

Published in Canada by
Somerville House Publishing
a division of Somerville House Books Limited
3080 Yonge Street, Suite 5000
Toronto, Ontario M4N 3N1

All photographs by Simon Bell with the exception of the following: owls, page 13: Johnny Johnson/Animals Animals; osprey, page 26: Robert Lankinen/First Light; and secretary birds, page 27: K&K Ammann/Masterfile.

The publisher and photographer would like to thank the following organizations and individuals without whose help this book would not have been possible: Metro Toronto Zoo, African Lion Safari, Alberta Birds of Prey Centre, Joseph Van OS Photo Safaris, Raptor Education Foundation, HawkQuest, Rock Mountain Raptor Center; special thanks to Toby Stiles, Wendy Slater, Perry Conway, Dr. Greg Hayes, Carol Precious, Heather Bell, and Joanne Harrison.

CONTENTS

INTRODUCING…BIRDS OF PREY	4
BIRDS OF PREY UP CLOSE	6
BIRD'S EYE VIEW	8
RAPTORS IN FLIGHT	10
FAMILY LIFE	12
OWLS EVERYWHERE	14
SIGHT AND SOUND	16
OWLS AT HOME	18
FALCONS AND HAWKS	20
FALCONS AT WORK	22
MAJESTIC EAGLES	24
MORE RAPTORS	26
NATURE'S CLEAN-UP CREW	28
STEREO PHOTOGRAPHY	30
GLOSSARY	31
INDEX	32

Words that appear in **bold** are explained in the glossary.

INTRODUCING... BIRDS OF PREY

- 3-D Gryrfalcon
- 3-D Bald Eagle
- 3-D Peregrine Falcon

▲ Burrowing owls can live in flat, treeless regions because they make their homes in abandoned holes dug by other animals, such as prairie dogs.

Birds that hunt for their food are called birds of **prey** or **raptors**. They use their powerful **talons** and sharp, curved beaks to catch and kill their prey.

These hunting birds belong to two groups: those who hunt for food in the daytime (**diurnal hunters**) and those who hunt at night (**nocturnal hunters**). Eagles, hawks, falcons, and vultures are daytime hunters. They belong to the order or group called *Falconiformes*. Owls, many of which are nighttime hunters, belong to the *Strigiformes* order.

Their oldest relative lived millions of years ago. It was called *Teratornis incredibilis*, a huge vulturelike bird with a wing span of over 17 feet (6 m).

Birds of prey are found all over the world. They live in many different types of **habitats**. Some perch high in the branches of trees, others live in open land. Some birds of prey have become less fearful of people and make their homes in barns or on the high ledges of buildings.

Raptors in Danger

All living things are part of **nature's food chain**. Each living species depends on other species to survive. When something disturbs this natural order, one or many populations suffer. For example, when insects destroy crops that are food for other living things, those species have nothing to eat and become scarce.

The barn owl, (see common barn owl card) like many birds of prey, helps keep the **rodent** and insect populations under control. When old trees and buildings are destroyed, these owls lose their homes and must search for new ones. Often, they move to another area, leaving the pest population to grow. This upsets the balance in nature. One way that farmers encourage helpful birds of prey, such as owls and kestrels, to live on their property is by building high perches and nesting boxes for them.

One of the greatest dangers to birds of prey are the poisonous chemicals that farmers spray on their fields to kill the insects and diseases that harm their crops. Raptors eat small animals and birds that feed on the seeds and plants grown in these fields. The poison from their prey remains in the raptors' bodies and causes them to die or have unhealthy babies. Today, with the use of less harmful **pesticides** and other conservation programs, these birds of prey have a better chance to survive and increase their numbers.

Peregrine falcons (see peregrine falcon card) almost became **extinct** in eastern North America in the 1960s because one of these chemicals, DDT, caused their egg shells to become very thin. When the mother peregrines sat on their eggs to keep them warm, the brittle shells broke and the unborn falcons died.

▲ Eagles prefer to live in remote areas far from humans. From high up in the mountains, this golden eagle (see golden eagle card) gazes over its homelands.

An Endangered Condor

By the 1980s, there were only about two dozen California condors, all living in captivity. Earlier, many of these large flying birds had been shot and others had died from being poisoned.

There are other threats to the condor that conservation programs cannot eliminate. Female condors lay only one egg every two years, so it takes a long time for the population to grow. Condors are not afraid of people and when these birds are released into their natural environment, they are attracted to populated areas – areas that present all sorts of dangers to these curious raptors.

BIRDS OF PREY UP CLOSE

- **3-D** Ferruginous Hawk
- **3-D** Black Hawk

You are most likely to see a bird of prey soaring majestically over a field, flying in slow circles, peering intently down at the ground for prey. Or you might see one in a high branch of a tree, patiently waiting for some prey to appear before swooping down quickly and catching it.

If you should see a raptor up close, you'll notice that they have distinctive beaks, talons, and eyes. But you may not notice them at all because raptors are able to hide themselves using clever **camouflage**.

Beaks

Birds of prey use their very strong, sharp, hooked beaks to tear apart their food. Hawks use their beaks to pluck the feathers from the small birds that they kill. Vultures and other scavenger birds rip the meat from the **carcasses** of dead animals with their sharp beaks.

▲ The kestrel's curved beak is strong and sharp, but not too large. Although kestrels eat mostly large insects, their beaks are perfectly adapted to pulling apart small **mammals**, **lizards and birds**.

▲ An owl's fluffy face feathers cover most of its beak, making it look quite small. The owl's mouth is really quite large so it can swallow its prey whole.

▲ The lappet-faced vulture has a strong, hooked beak that is perfect for tearing open the thick hides of large, dead animals.

Talons

Birds of prey have four powerful toes with sharp claws called talons on each foot. They use these powerful talons to grip and kill their prey. Some hunters have long middle toes that they use like spears to catch their prey in flight. Birds of prey who hunt fish or snakes have rough scales on their toes so these animals can't get away. Owls and ospreys can twist one toe to the back of their foot when grasping prey. This special revolving toe gives these raptors a particularly firm grip.

▶ **The Swainson's hawk's** (see Swainson's hawk card) talons are long and curved, perfect for grasping small animals. Hawks that catch birds have longer legs and thinner toes than those that catch mammals.

▶ **The barn owl thrusts its feet forward and moves its revolving toe to the back of its foot as it closes in to capture its meal. It spreads its wings at the last moment to prevent itself from crashing into the ground.**

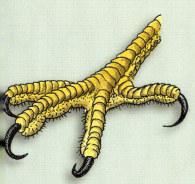

▲ The undersides of a fish eagle's feet are spiny for gripping its slippery prey.

▲ The monkey-eating eagle's large feet have a powerful grasp.

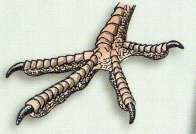

▲ Since a vulture rarely has to hold a struggling prey, its feet are much weaker and its talons are much blunter than an eagle's are.

BIRD'S EYE VIEW

3-D **Prairie Falcon**
3-D **King Vulture**

Sight

Most birds of prey have eyes that are large compared to the size of their heads. These large, slightly flat eyes allow the bird to see objects that are only a blur to us.

All birds of prey, except for owls, have eyes that are close to the sides of their heads. They can look out of one eye at a time and move their eyes separately. In this way, they can keep a careful watch on two different places at the same time! As soon as one eye spots prey, the bird turns its head and looks in the prey's direction with both eyes to judge how far away it is. With their keen eyesight, these hunters can spot their food from far off and then swoop down swiftly and catch their unsuspecting victim.

▶ The great horned owl turns its head almost in a circle to see behind. Since owls hunt mostly at night, their eyesight and hearing are keen. This helps them find their prey in the dark.

Hearing and Smell

Most birds of prey rely on their sense of sight more than their other senses. However, some raptors use hearing or smell as well as sight to spot their prey. Because owls hunts at night, they have very acute hearing so they can pinpoint the exact position of their prey. The king vulture lives in the dense rain forest and rarely can see its prey. This vulture's sensitive sense of smell helps it find rotting carcasses among the plants on the rain forest's floor.

Coloring

Few birds of prey are colorful. An exception is the king vulture (see king vulture card), which lives in the rain forests of Central and South America. In these dark, green jungles, camouflage is not as important for this large bird, which has few enemies. The bird is easy to see, with its black and white **plumage** and colorful head.

Although most female and male birds of prey have similar coloring, in some types, such as kestrels, the male coloring is somewhat brighter. Newly hatched birds of prey can look very different from their parents. As young birds of prey mature, they often go through different stages of coloring. Bald eagles, for example, don't develop their distinctive white heads until they are about four years old.

▶ The bald eagle (see bald eagle card) is not bald at all – its head is covered with pure white feathers. This bird's name comes from the Old English word "balde," meaning "white."

RAPTORS IN FLIGHT

Birds of prey, like all flying birds, have a body structure that is lightweight but powerful. They have hollow bones to keep their bodies light enough for flying. Their skeletons are structured in a way that make the birds very strong for capturing and carrying their food.

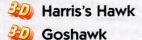

3-D Harris's Hawk
3-D Goshawk

You can often tell how a bird flies by looking at the shape of its wings and tail. Eagles and vultures have long, broad wings that help them soar through the air. Birds of prey that live in wooded areas often have rounded wings and long tails so they can fly accurately among the trees.

By flapping its pointed wings rapidly, the kestrel can hover like a helicopter as it searches for food on the ground. To do this, the bird fans its tail and angles itself into the wind for balance. Birds that sit on high perches, such as tree branches and poles, also use their tails for balance.

The goshawk (see northern goshawk card) is a skilled forest flyer. Although its wings are quite long for a forest bird, they are rounded and perfectly suited for whizzing through the trees and making sudden turns. The goshawk's tail is long, like that of other forest-dwelling birds.

The larger birds of prey are among the biggest flying birds in the world. Some birds of prey, like the Andean condor, wouldn't be able to get off the ground if they were any larger.

◀ **The eye sockets in the skeleton of a bird of prey are unusually large and set close together.**

How Raptors Feed

Many birds of prey catch enough food at one time to last for the whole day. Except for owls, birds of prey have a pouch inside their bodies called a **crop**. In it, they store the food to eat later or to feed their babies.

Some birds of prey are **scavengers** and do very little hunting. Vultures feed on dead animals called **carrion**. These scavengers are useful in cleaning up decaying carcasses that could spread disease.

In winter, when it is difficult to find food, eagles scavenge for carrion, much like vultures. Some eagles attack other birds in mid-flight to steal their food. The bald eagle winters near river beds to feed on salmon after they swim up river to lay their eggs.

▲ This golden eagle billows its wings as it lands on a branch. The eagle's wings act like a parachute, slowing its descent so it doesn't crash.

▼ The red-tailed hawk uses its fan-like tail to balance on a perch. Its wide tail and long, broad wings are typical of hawks who soar when looking for prey.

A Tasty Meal

Hunting birds, especially those that swallow their food whole, often can't digest some parts of their prey. This waste material, mainly bones, fur and feathers, forms into a tight little **pellet** that the bird coughs up and spits out. By examining the pellet, scientists can determine what the bird ate and which parts of its prey the bird digests as food.

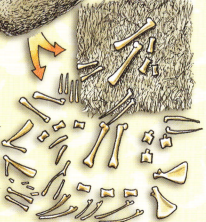

FAMILY LIFE

3-D Northern Harrier
3-D Eagle Owl

Most birds of prey make good parents. Year after year, many return to the same nest to lay their eggs and hatch their babies. Usually, the female stays in the nest while the male hunts for food. Even after the young birds learn to fly, the family may stay together for several weeks or even months. Only the strong survive, so these young birds must learn to hunt before they are ready to be on their own.

Eggs and Hatchlings

The number of eggs that different species lay ranges from one egg every other year, as is the case with the condor, to several during each mating season. Some birds of prey lay one egg each day or one every other day, so the babies hatch over several days or even weeks. When food is scarce, the older babies are stronger and usually can survive, while the younger ones often die.

Since birds of prey must be skillful hunters to survive, the young birds must learn to hunt before they leave home. The parent eagle seems to play games with its young to train it to snatch its prey quickly. While the young eagle is flying, the parent bird circles above and drops a morsel of food for the youngster to catch.

▼ Because it is such a large bird, the golden eagle's (see golden eagle card) eggs are much larger than the eggs of other birds of prey. The gyrfalcon's (see gyrfalcon card) egg is a mottled brown, while the barn owl's (see common barn owl card) egg is small and white.

golden eagle egg

gyrfalcon egg

barn owl egg

Most birds of prey have only one mate each season. The harrier (see northern harrier card) is an exception. Some male harriers have to find food for two or three families. Instead of delivering the food to the nest, the male harrier calls to the female. She flies toward the male. He drops the food and she catches it in mid-air with her talons.

▲ The young of the great horned owl spend about two weeks hopping from branch to branch or scurrying on the ground while they are learning to fly. This is called branching. The owlets also flap their wings to make them strong.

OWLS EVERYWHERE

 Screech Owl
 Long-eared Owl

Owls can be found almost everywhere — from hot tropical forests to the frozen Arctic tundra. Owls usually remain in the same area all their lives. Many owls live in trees, while others live in marshlands, prairies, and even in burrows in the ground.

You are much more likely to hear an owl than to see one because the owl's feathers match its surroundings. This camouflage protects the owl from its enemies while it sleeps during the day, waiting for night to begin its hunting.

Silent Hunters

Owls are superb hunters. Their bodies are uniquely adapted to helping them hunt. They swoop down without a sound, grip their prey with their powerful toes and sharp talons, and kill it with their pointed, curved beak, which can open wide enough to swallow most prey whole. Owls eat mainly mice, voles, shrews, and snakes, though some owls eat other birds and larger animals, such as rabbits, porcupines, skunks, and foxes.

Although owls do not fly very fast, they fly silently, catching their prey by surprise. Other birds make a whooshing sound with their wings, but these silent hunters could fly right past your ear without you hearing a sound. Their wings are long and surprisingly light, but very strong so that they can lift the weight of their prey and carry it back to their nest.

◀ The barred owl's (see barred owl card) feathers blend in with the color of the tree bark and make it difficult to see.

Fluffy Feathers

Owl feathers are much softer than those of other birds of prey. Their feathers give them a fluffy appearance. Owls living in cold climates have a warm layer of **down** (very fine, warm feathers) under their feathers. An owl's wing feather has a fringed edge that allows air to pass silently through its wings as it flies.

For thousands of years, people have been fascinated by owls. In ancient times, many thought owls were spirits with magic powers. Athena, the Greek goddess of wisdom, was sometimes depicted with the head of an owl or with an owl sitting on her shoulder.

▼ A great horned owl takes off from its perch. As it spreads its huge wings, its large feet hang below, displaying its sharp talons.

SIGHT AND SOUND

3-D **Barn Owl**
3-D **Barred Owl**

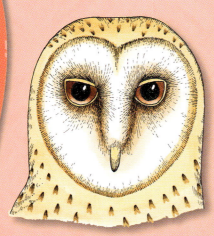

▲ A barn owl displays its facial disk.

▶ This short-eared owl has quickly turned its head to investigate a sound coming from behind.

Looking Around

An owl's eyes look straight ahead so that it can accurately judge distance and depth. Its eyes can focus very quickly so it can see close and distant objects at the same time. The owl cannot roll its eyes or see to the sides without turning its head, but its extremely flexible neck allows it to look backwards while its body is facing forward. In this way, the owl can silently spot its prey without moving very much.

Satellite Hearing

Owls have a circle of long, soft feathers, called the *facial disk*, surrounding their eyes and extending from the rims of the ear slits. Like a television satellite dish, the facial disk captures sounds and sends them into the owl's ears.

The owl's excellent hearing allows it to locate exactly where its prey is, even in the dark. The owl's ear slits are placed at different positions on each side of its head. The right ear is higher and hears sounds from above. The left ear is lower and can pick up noises below the owl's perch. These special ears help the owl locate the exact position of a sound.

More Than a Hoot

Owls have more to say than just "hoot." They snort and screech. They "meow" like a hungry cat and "ting" like a dripping faucet. Owls even whine, whistle, and scream!

When male owls are looking for a mate they hoot loudly. An interested female replies with a different call. The male continues to hoot to the shy female until she is comfortable and returns his mating call. Then, the mating couple often sing together.

Keeping Out of Sight

Owls are not very easily seen because their feathers are the color of their surroundings. An owl's feathers are usually brown or gray or a mix of the two colors. Young owls often change color as they grow. Their bodies are covered with soft gray down feathers until their adult flying feathers grow in.

The flammulated owl's (see flammulated owl card) feathers are like flames of cinnamon and silver and blend nicely into the bark of trees. But, unlike other birds, the flammulated owl uses its call to help its camouflage. This little owl throws its voice, sending its predator to look for it in the wrong place!

▼ When an owl feels threatened, it will puff up its feathers, making it look twice its actual size. This annoyed eagle owl (see eagle owl card) looks menacing.

OWLS AT HOME

3-D Snowy Owl
3-D Spectacled Owl

Family Life

Most owls live alone in their own territories until breeding season. At that time, a male owl presents a female with a dead mouse or other prey to show her that he is a good provider and to persuade her to become his mate.

If the male is successful, he brings the female to the nest that he has chosen (often the abandoned nest of another bird). There she lays eggs several days apart over a period of a week or two. For the next three weeks, the female keeps the eggs warm with her body while the male gathers food. Once the owlets are born, both parents hunt for food.

At first, they must tear the prey apart and feed it in small pieces to the noisy, hungry owlets, but soon the young ones are able to do this for themselves. Feeding the babies is very hard work. In just one season, a pair of owls must kill hundreds of rodents to feed their owlets and themselves.

Owlets cannot fly until they have developed a full set of feathers. It also takes them some months to learn to be skilled hunters, so owl families often stay together through the first winter. While the mother is off in search of food, barn owlets look after one another. The older ones keep the younger owlets warm and may even try to feed them. But this doesn't happen in all owl families. If there is a shortage of food, some older owlets kill the younger ones.

▶ A barn owl (see common barn owl card) has captured a mouse. She will take it back to her nest to feed her owlets.

In this way, only the strongest owlets survive. Owls are often poor housekeepers. They seldom clean their nests, which are littered with bits of food and droppings. Although snakes are among their favorite meals, eastern screech owls will sometimes capture a small blind snake and keep it alive in the nest to clean up the litter.

Snowy Owls

The snowy owl (see snowy owl card) is well adapted to life in a snow-covered, treeless, rocky **environment**. This large bird's thick feathers keep it warm and help it to hide in its surroundings. The male, which is almost completely white, blends in easily with the snow. The female, covered in dark speckles, is difficult to spot among the rocks that hold her nest.

The snowy owl is the only owl that can store body fat. This extra supply lets it survive the long winter when the weather makes it impossible to hunt. In the Arctic summer, daylight hours are so long that the snowy owl cannot wait for darkness to hunt. It is a powerful hunter.

Snowy owls feed mainly on **lemmings**, and the female owl lays more or fewer eggs, depending on whether or not there is an adequate supply of lemmings. If lemmings are scarce, snowy owls migrate to southern regions in search of food.

The Spectacled Owl

The spectacled owl (see spectacled owl card) lives in the mangrove swamps and rain forests of Central and South America. This odd-looking bird is dark brown and white. A striking pattern on its face looks like a pair of glasses. Young spectacled owls are bright white, so they don't blend in with their surroundings at all. In Brazil, the spectacled owl is called the "knocking bird," because its call sounds just like the hammering of a woodpecker.

▲ The snowy owl's soft leg feathers protect it from frostbite during the cold winter weather.

▲ Owlets huddle together waiting for a parent to bring them food.

FALCONS AND HAWKS

Falcons and hawks, two very similar kinds of birds of prey, can be found on every continent except Antarctica. They are daytime hunting birds with strong, hooked beaks and sharp talons. Both of these raptors are strong and spectacular fliers.

3-D Swainson's Harrier
3-D Northern Goshawk

Hunting Habits

Falcons and hawks differ in the way they kill their prey. With their keen eyesight, falcons spot their prey from far away and sweep down with great speed to catch it by surprise. These steep descents are called **stoops**. Most falcons rush straight toward the prey and bite it on the head or neck. Sometimes the force is so strong that they bite the head right off! Hawks pull back

▼ The Harris's hawk (see Harris's hawk card) holds its wings forward around its food as it eats. This "mantle" of feathers disguises its meal from other hungry birds.

their wings just before they make contact so they can use their sharp talons to grab and kill their prey.

Falcons and hawks are known to be creative hunters. Many of them have developed clever tricks to complement their hunting skill. Swainson's hawks (see Swainson's hawk card) usually watch for prey from a perch. But sometimes they fly behind a farm tractor as it works the soil in a field. As rodents and insects are exposed in the up-turned soil, the Swainson's hawk swoops down and grabs an easy meal.

Different Names

All falcons are called *falcos* but there are two types of hawks. There are **accipiters**, such as the goshawk (see northern goshawk card), who watch for their prey from high, stationary positions, such as telephone poles. Accipiters have long tails and short wings. They prey mainly on smaller birds. For this reason, they are also called bird hawks.

Other types of hawks are called **buteos**. They glide through the air in circles while hunting. Buteos have wider tails and longer wings than accipiters. They are also called *buzzards* or *buzzard hawks*. Buteos tend to eat mammals, snakes, and sometimes large insects.

Family Life

Some hawks build elaborate nests of twigs and grass while others scrape a clearing on a protected cliff or high spot to make a home for their young. It is usually the female's role to sit on the eggs until they hatch. Sometimes the father will help but his main job is providing food for his family. When the young hawks have grown a warm coat of feathers, the mother leaves the nest to hunt for food.

Instead of building their own nests, falcons lay their eggs almost anywhere — in old trees, on building ledges, or in the old nests of other birds. The parents take turns sitting on the eggs, keeping them warm until they hatch. Although the young birds can fly within six weeks, their parents continue to feed them for several months.

▲ **This Harris's hawk glides low, scouring the ground for unwary prey.**

FALCONS AT WORK

3-D American Kestrel
3-D African Fish Eagle

Peregrine Falcons

Peregrine falcons are the fastest birds in the world. They can reach speeds of up to 110 miles (180 km) per hour as they make a steep dive towards their prey. Their bodies are about 20 inches (50 cm) long and are designed for speed.

When they dive, their shape resembles a bullet. Peregrines even have special **deflectors** in their nostrils to prevent air from rushing into their lungs too quickly as they dive. The falcon closes off its nasal passage when it folds into a stoop to dive at prey.

Many falcons capture their food on the ground, but the peregrine (see peregrine falcon card) also captures its prey in mid-air. With its speed, it kills with a single blow from its hind toe. Peregrines tend to live in high areas, such as cliffs near water, mountains, or even city skyscrapers.

▲ Falcons, like this gyrfalcon, tend to have more distinctive plumage than other birds of prey.

▲ Four steps of a falcon's stoop.

Kestrels

Kestrels are the most common and the smallest members of the falcon family. The male has gray-blue wings and its back is reddish-brown with dark speckles. The female is almost entirely reddish-brown.

Kestrels live in diverse habitats, from pastures to cities. The common kestrel is about 13-15 inches (33-40 cm), and ranges through Africa, Asia, and Europe. It eats insects, lizards, and small birds. The American kestrel (see American kestrel card) is about 10.5 inches (27 cm) long, the size of a blue jay. It ranges from South America to Alaska, and usually eats insects.

The kestrel is also called a wind hoverer, because it **hovers** above the ground as it looks for food. A kestrel can fly in one spot, even in high winds.

Falconry - A Noble Sport

Gyrfalcons (see gyrfalcon card), the largest of the falcons, have white or gray feathers with black speckles and tips. They are often used for the sport of **falconry**, where they are trained to hunt other birds and then return to the falconer's hand. In the Middle Ages, only kings were allowed to use gyrfalcons for falconry, because these birds were considered to be the most majestic falcons.

MAJESTIC EAGLES

- 3-D Bald Eagle
- 3-D Golden Eagle
- 3-D African Fish Eagle

▲ A bald eagle (see bald eagle card) prepares for flight.

Eagles are excellent hunters. With their keen eyesight, they can spot prey from long distances and kill it quickly with their strong talons. Although they can kill large animals such as piglets and small antelopes, most eagles prefer to capture prey that they can carry to a safe eating place. When food is scarce, eagles will eat carrion. The African fish eagle will steal food from other birds of prey, including its own mate, even when it isn't hungry!

As they fly, eagles glide gracefully through the air. They ride the winds and air currents, hardly needing to flap their huge wings at all. Eagles will often fly over 200 miles (320 km) in one day.

The largest eagles have wing spans of over 6 feet (2 m). Eagles' wings turn up at the ends and are deeply slotted, almost like fingers. These slots reduce the drag on the wing, helping the eagle soar.

Respected Raptor

An eagle circling slowly, silently, overhead is a majestic sight. Eagles have symbolized power and freedom in many different cultures. These regal birds have graced flags and royal coats of arms for thousands of years. The golden eagle was the emblem of the army of the Roman Empire, and the bald eagle is the national bird of the United States. When an eagle circles above a Native American ceremony, it is considered a great blessing because eagles are considered to be the messengers of the spirits.

Territorial Birds

Some eagles' homes are spread over huge territories. For example, the golden eagle has a territory of up to 400 square miles (1,100 km^2).

Eagles mark their territories by performing spectacular aerial acrobatics and squawking loudly. Other birds of prey are considered intruders and will be challenged, if not attacked.

Eagles start mating when they are about four years old, and keep the same partner for life, usually another 20 years. While the female sits on the eggs, the male brings her food. Once the eggs hatch, the parents take turns guarding the nest and searching for food for the eaglets. Although two eggs hatch, often only one baby eagle will survive. The more aggressive eaglet takes most of the food, and often attacks its **sibling**, sometimes killing it.

Golden Eagle

The golden eagle (see golden eagle card), the largest of all eagles is a fierce-looking bird with beautiful plumage. If a golden eagle ruffles its feathers — watch out! It is trying to scare you away by making itself look larger, and if that doesn't work, its next move will be to strike!

The golden eagle is an **agile** hunter and can dive at very high speeds. When it spots a meal, usually a rabbit or large rodent, the prey does not have much chance of escaping. The golden eagle swoops down feet first. It grasps the prey with its three forward-facing toes, and stabs the victim with its dagger-like back talon. It easily tears its prey to pieces with its two-inch long hooked beak.

▶ **The setting sun highlights this golden eagle's plumage.**

Huge Homes

Eagles build nests high up on secluded cliff ledges, or at the top of tall trees. Branches make up most of the nest, with a lining of leaves or feathers to keep the eaglets warm and comfortable. The nests are called **eyries**. Some eagles use them year after year, adding new nesting material. The eyries built in trees get larger, and heavier, and then — snap! — the supporting branch breaks, and the nest falls to the ground.

MORE RAPTORS

3-D Flammulated Owl

Osprey

The osprey is a fishing bird that is found near water throughout the world. Many of the osprey's physical features are especially suited for fishing. Its talons have spiny undersides to help it grip slippery fish. One of its four toes revolves, so it can grasp a squirming fish with two toes on each side. The osprey's feathers are shorter and oilier than those of other birds of prey. These special feathers **repel** water, so the osprey doesn't become so wet and heavy that it can't fly.

The osprey is a powerful hunter. It flies slowly above the water, scanning below the water surface for prey. When the osprey sees a fish, it hovers, takes aim, and dives feet first at the fish. With a huge splash, the osprey hits the water, and rises with the fish in its talons. As it flies, the osprey shakes its feathers like a wet dog, and adjusts its strong grip around the fish. Sometimes the osprey's grip is too powerful. A large fish can pull an osprey underwater, and drown a bird that refuses to let go.

◀ **An osprey prepares to eat a fish it has caught and brought back to its nest.**

Kite

Kites can live in a variety of habitats because of their diet. They attack and eat living prey, but they also eat rotting food and garbage. Many European species of this large bird of prey will eat carrion, including the "road kill" found on highways. Kites enjoy eating fish, so they often build nests near water — but high up, at least 30 feet (9 m) above ground. Kites living in the Americas have varied diets: some eat primarily insects, others eat rodents, some eat snails — and some eat just about anything.

European kites live in northern Europe in the summer and then fly to Africa for the winter. Kites are fast fliers, traveling up to 560 miles (900 km) in one day.

▲ Everglade kites will only dine on snails. Their beaks are long and curved – perfect for pulling their favorite meal from its shell.

Secretary Bird

The secretary bird is an unusual and interesting raptor that lives in the grasslands of Africa. It has a brightly colored face and eyelashes that can be an inch (2.5 cm) long! Although it can fly, the secretary bird prefers to run on its long, thin legs and may walk as far as 20 miles (32 km) a day looking for food. This bird catches small mammals, such as rats and tortoises, with its large feet and kicks them to death! It is famous for catching snakes, which it spears with the talon on its back toe. The tough scales on its legs and feet protect the secretary bird from poisonous snake bites.

When the male is looking for a mate, he does a dance on the ground and performs spectacular dives and turns as he flies. These birds choose the top of flat-topped trees to build their nests. The female lays only two eggs and the parents take turns guarding the nest and hunting for food.

Why is it called "secretary bird"? Legend has it that the name comes from the long feathers on its head that look like the bird has a quill pen tucked behind its ear. The name is actually a mispronunciation of the bird's Arabic name, *sagr al-tēr*, which means "hawk birds."

▲ Secretary birds perform a courting ritual.

NATURE'S CLEAN-UP CREW

3-D Turkey Vulture
3-D Cinereous Vulture

When predators kill other animals, they do not eat everything — so vultures finish the leftovers. They eat the flesh of dead animals before it starts to rot.

Vultures look quite different from other birds of prey. They are well adapted to be scavengers. Their long skinny necks make it easy for them to reach deep inside a carcass. Feathers on a vulture's head and neck would get very bloody when feeding, so most vultures are bald. One vulture, the turkey vulture, gets its name because its bright red head looks similar to a turkey's head.

With their excellent eyesight, vultures are able to see carrion from great distances. Their talons are much weaker than those of other birds of prey. Since vultures do not usually kill their own prey, they do not need a strong grip.

However, they have powerful beaks for ripping the flesh from the bones of dead animals. Although it is not common, vultures will sometimes scare small animals over the edges of cliffs, and then feed on the dead body.

▲ The colorful king vulture (see king vulture card) has a well-developed sense of smell to help it find carcasses in the dense rain forest.

No Manners!

A meal around a carcass is hardly a civilized event. There is a great deal of squabbling. A vulture determined to get a good place at the carcass will extend its wings, point its toes outwards, and leap at the other vultures, hissing loudly. Sometimes vultures eat so much, they can't fly away! Once a vulture has finished its meal, all it really wants is a bath. Vultures will fly a very long way to find some water to wash up after their gory meal.

Ready for Take-off

Vultures are heavy birds, and some, like the California condor, have difficulty taking off from a standing position. The larger vultures will fly from trees or cliffs, falling into flight, rather than lifting off. Often, condors must find a runway. A grassy slope will do. They run as fast as they can and then jump into the air. Once in the air, vultures glide effortlessly on their huge wings. With the help of upward currents of air called **thermals**, vultures can reach incredible heights, often disappearing from sight.

Home Life

Vultures are very careful and caring parents. Most vultures have only one baby each season, so if that young bird dies, the parents will have to wait a full year before they can have another. Vulture eggs are incubated for 39-50 days and the young vulture remains in the nest for three to seven months. At first, the mother stays with the young vulture and the father brings them both food. Later, both parents leave the nest to search for food. The youngsters are quite safe in the nest alone because their nests are difficult to find.

The Egyptian Vulture

Ostrich eggs are one of the Egyptian vulture's favorite meals, but the bird's small, thin beak is suited to picking at bones, not cracking thick-shelled eggs. Egyptian vultures have learned to use tools in securing their food. When this vulture finds an ostrich egg, it picks up small stones and flings them at the egg. Once the shell cracks, the vulture slurps up the tasty yolk.

▲ The cinereous vulture (see cinereous vulture card) is an aggressive bird. It will drive all other vultures away from carrion. It is among the largest vultures in Africa, Asia, and Europe, living in mountainous areas, including the Himalayas.

STEREO PHOTOGRAPHY

Our Eyes

A pair of eyes is one of the most complex systems found in nature. Scientists don't fully understand all the intricate mechanisms that allow humans and animals to see. Scientists do know, however, that both eyes work together with the brain to form images that have three dimensions: length, width, and depth. Viewed through only one eye, everything appears flat, or two-dimensional. Using two eyes allows humans to perceive the third dimension—depth.

How the Eyes Work

Because our eyes are a few inches apart, each eye sees a slightly different angle of the same object. The information from each eye is carried by nerves to the brain. Then, in a process called fusion, the brain forms a blended image that is three-dimensional. Fusion allows humans to judge distances between objects, and determine how far away they are.

How a Stereo Camera Works

Stereophotography works like human eyesight. The most sophisticated stereo cameras have two lenses about the same distance apart as human eyes. Two images are taken simultaneously, each with a slightly different angle of the same object. When both images are viewed through a special viewer, called a stereoscope, the two images are blended together to become one image that has three dimensions.

Eye-to-Eye™ Books

This Eye-to-Eye™ book contains cards with paired images of birds of prey taken by a stereo camera. When you look at the cards through the stereoscopic viewer, a 3-D image is formed in your brain. This is because the left side of the card mimics what the left eye might see, while the right side mimics the right eye's perspective.

To View the Cards

Carefully remove the viewer from the front of the book. Lift flap and insert tab. Carefully remove the cards from the back of the book. Insert cards one by one into the slot. When you have finished viewing the cards, store the viewer and cards in the pocket on the inside back cover.

Simon M. Bell specializes in stereographic nature photography and is founder and president of BPS, a multimedia studio based in Toronto, Canada.

Simon began shooting pictures at the age of six when his father gave him a "Brownie" box camera.

GLOSSARY

Accipiters - any of a class of small and medium-sized hawks having relatively short, rounded wings, and a long tail.
Agile - capable of moving swiftly and easily.
Buteo - a kind of hawk with a thick-set body, broad wings, and a short, broad tail. Found in many parts of the world, buteos will soar high in the air for hours while hunting.
Camouflage - the natural coloring of an animal that enables it to blend in with its surroundings and hide from predators.
Carcass - the dead body of an animal.
Carrion - dead and decaying flesh.
Crop - a pouch in the neck of a bird where food is stored and partially digested.
Deflector - something that causes a change from a straight course or fixed direction.
Diurnal hunters - hunters who hunt during the daytime.
Down - fine, soft, fluffy feathers.
Environment - the surroundings in which a plant or animal lives.
Extinct - no longer in existence.

Eyrie (or **aerie**)- the nest of a bird on a cliff or mountaintop.
Falconry - the art of training falcons to pursue game; the sport of hunting with falcons.
Habitats - the places or kinds of places where an animal or plant usually lives or grows.
Hatchlings - a recently hatched bird or animal.
Hover - stay in one place in the air; float or fly without moving much.
Lemmings - a type of small, short-tailed, furry-footed Arctic rodent. They are notable for mass migrations which often continue into the sea where many of them are drowned.
Mammals - animals that have four legs, fur, or hair, and the ability among females to produce milk for their young.
Menacing - threatening; likely to inflict harm.
Nature's food chain - a system in nature in which each predatory species uses the next, usually lower member as a food source.
Nocturnal hunters - hunters that hunt at night.
Pellet - a very small, hard ball made of different substances.

Pesticide - any chemical or other substance used to destroy plant or animal pests.
Plumage - the feathers of a bird.
Predator - an animal that lives by killing and eating other animals.
Prey - an animal caught or hunted by another animal for food.
Raptor - a bird of prey.
Repel - to keep off or out; resist.
Rodent - any of several related animals, such as a mouse, rat, squirrel, or beaver. Rodents have large front teeth used for gnawing.
Scavenger - an animal that feeds on dead animals or other decaying matter.
Sibling - a brother or sister.
Stoop - the descent of a hawk on its prey.
Talon - the claw of an animal or bird that seizes other animals as prey.
Thermal - a bubble, or column, of rising air currents that are warmer than the surrounding air. Thermals are used by gliders to gain altitude.

INDEX

Entries in *italics* refer to photographs and illustrations.

Accipiters, 21
African fish eagle, 22, 24
American kestrel, 22, 23
Andean condor, 10
Baby owls, 19
bald eagle, 4, 9, 11, 24
barn owl, 4, 7, 16, 18
barred owl, 14, 16
beak, 6, 14, 20, 25, 27, 28, 29
bird hawks, 21
black hawk, 6
burrowing owl, 4
buteos, 21
buzzards, 21
California condor, 5, 29
cinereous vulture, 28, 29
common kestrel, 23
condor, 5, 10, 12, 29
Eagle owl, 12, 17
eagles, 4-5, 7, 9, 10, 11, 12, 24-25
ears, 16
eastern screech owls, 19
eggs, 12, 18, 21, 25, 29
Egyptian vulture, 29
European kites, 27
Everglade kites, 27
eyes, 6, 8, 16

eyesight
 of eagles, 24
 of owls, 8
 of vultures, 28
Facial disk, 16
falconry, 23
falcons, 4-5, 12, 20-23, 25
feathers, 6, 9, 14, 15, 17, 19, 20, 21, 23, 26, 27, 28
ferruginous hawk, 6
fish eagle, 7
flammulated owl, 17, 26
Golden eagle, 5, 11, 12, 24, 25
goshawk, 10, 20
great horned owl, 8, 13, 15
gyrfalcon, 4, 12, 22, 23
Harrier, 13
Harris's hawk, 10, 20, 21
hawks, 4, 6, 7, 11, 20-21
hearing of owls, 8, 16
Kestrels, 4, 6, 9, 10, 22-23
king vulture, 8, 9, 28
kites, 27
Lappet-faced vulture, 6
long-eared owl, 14
Monkey-eating eagle, 7
Northern goshawk, 20

northern harrier, 12
Ospreys, 7, 26
owls, 4, 6, 7, 8, 9, 11, 14-19
Peregrine falcon, 4, 5, 22
plumage. *See* Feathers.
prairie falcon, 8
Red-tailed hawk, 11
Screech owl, 14
secretary bird, 26, 27
sense of hearing, 9
sense of sight, 9
sense of smell, 9
short-eared owl, 16
skeleton, 10
snowy owl, 18, 19
spectacled owl, 18, 19
Swainson's harrier, 20
Swainson's hawk, 7, 21
Tails, 10, 11, 21
talons, 6, 7, 11, 13, 14, 15, 20, 22, 24, 25, 26, 27, 28
toes. *See* talons.
turkey vulture, 28
Vultures, 4, 6, 7, 9, 10, 11, 28-29
Wind hoverer, 23
wings, 10, 11, 14, 20, 21, 22, 24, 28